CLEAR MIND

A GOAL SETTING WORKBOOK FOR AGILITY HANDLERS

SHAWNA L. PALMER, PH.D.
DAISY PEEL, M.SC.

Pinnacle Performance International, LLC
Bellevue, WA 98006

Copyright © 2011 Pinnacle Performance, LLC
Print Edition, 2011
eBook Edition, 2011

IMPORTANT

ISBN
978-0-9832780-2-3 (Print)
978-0-9832780-1-6 (eBook)

Published in the United States of America

DISCLAIMER

This book is designed to provide information on goal setting and how to integrate related skills into regular physical training. If other expert assistance is required, the services of a competent professional should be sought. It is the purpose of this manual to complement existing sources of information on this topic. You are urged to read all the available material, learn as much as possible about the topic, and tailor the information to your individual needs. Every effort has been made to make this manual as complete and as accurate as possible. The purpose of this manual is to educate. The authors shall have neither liability nor responsibility to any person or entity with respect to any loss or damage caused, or alleged to have been caused, directly or indirectly, by the information contained in this book. If you do not wish to be bound by the above, you may return this book to the publisher for a full refund.

ACKNOWLEDGEMENTS: PHOTOS

Photography by M (Front cover, left; Back cover, D.P.)
PhotographybyM.com

Northwest Dog Shots (Front cover, top)
nwdogshots.com

Mike Lifer Photography (Front cover, bottom right)
mlifer.com

Clear Mind

ABOUT THE AUTHORS

Shawna Palmer has a Masters degree in Sports Psychology and a Ph.D. in Neuropsychology. She has served as consultant to many athletes, in a number of sports and at all levels, from the novice to the international competitor. Shawna has also presented sports psychology seminars and education sessions to coaches, clubs and sport organizations in multiple countries, emphasizing personal achievement and psychological skill building that integrates seamlessly into daily training programs. Shawna also knows dog agility from a handler's point of view, competing in AKC and USDAA events with her young dog Jedi, qualifying for national level competition during her first year.

Daisy Peel currently teaches classes and trains in Sumner, Washington, teaches seminars worldwide, and has competed at the highest levels of agility competition. She has a Bachelor's degree in chemistry and a Masters degree in Science Education. Daisy began agility in 1998, and in 2006, Daisy and her rescue border collie Fly were Reserve National Champions at the AKC National

Agility Championship in Tampa, Florida. Goal setting and mental management skills did not come easily to Daisy, and she has worked hard to improve her skills over the years. As a result, her performances improved dramatically. Daisy and her dog Jester won the AKC National Agility Championship in Sunbury Ohio, and went on to compete at the 2007 FCI World Agility Championships in Hamar, Norway. Most recently, Daisy and her young dog Solar won a spot on the 2011 AKC FCI World Agility Team for the second time (in 2010 they were named to the 2010 AKC FCI World Agility Team, and took 6th overall at the 2010 FCI Agility World Championships). Daisy and her dogs have been National Finalists over eighteen times, and she has been a National Champion four times (AKC/USDAA). Daisy's interest in the mental aspect of the sport of dog agility was sparked early on, when it became clear that she needed to move fast, but think faster!

Shawna and Daisy believe that physical skill is simply not enough – to reach your fullest potential, strong and positive mental preparation must accompany the performance and setting effective principle-based goals is the first step in your mental preparation.

FOREWORD
BY LINDA MECKLENBURG

O ver the years, I've done my best to help many agility handlers achieve their dreams. Most handlers recognize the need to prepare for agility competition by training their dogs and improving their handling skills. However, handlers often overlook the importance of mental preparation and how it can affect performance.

When a student initially comes to me for agility instruction or coaching, my first question is, "What are your goals?" A surprising number of handlers have never stopped to consider what their goals are. Clear Mind will help you as an agility handler understand the importance of goal setting and show you how to outline a plan for meeting those goals.

Prior to dog agility, I competed in equestrian events. It was common practice to periodically give the horses a break from competition and "turn them out to pasture". This gave the horses some rest from the physical rigors of competition and they returned to the ring mentally refreshed as well. The transition back to competition was gradual starting with a review of simple skills, followed by a steady progression in the level of difficulty of the performances, culminating in a challenging top-level event where superior performance was desired. Clear Mind describes how to apply a similar strategy to training in dog agility.

These are two aspects of positive mental preparation described in Clear Mind. With Shawna's background in both sports psychology plus dog agility, and Daisy's competitive experience in agility plus education, the authors are uniquely qualified to write a book on mental preparation. Clear Mind is currently one of the few resources available to agility enthusiasts that focuses on this aspect of performance.

I encourage all handlers to take advantage of the step-by-step guidance Clear Mind provides in order to help you achieve your dreams in agility. Whether you run agility for recreation or aspire to compete against the best in the sport, your performance will benefit if you formulate a solid plan for the present and develop an understanding of how to continue setting the most effective goals for years to come. Clear Mind gives you the tools to do just that. Enjoy!

Linda Mecklenburg, Author
Developing Handling Skills
Developing Jumping Skills
www.awesomepaws.us

Contents

CONTENTS CONTINUED

INTRODUCTION
BY DAISY PEEL

When I got started in dog agility, over ten years ago, my experience as an athlete was limited to playing clarinet in the marching band at high school and University. I didn't like sports, had never played a sport, and couldn't understand why some people seemed to be consumed by training and preparing for the sports they played. The only competitions I had participated in were spelling bees as an elementary school student, and the only preparation I did for that was to read a lot of books....something I enjoyed doing anyway!

During my senior year in college, I saw a television show about dog agility and was hooked. I wanted a dog, and I wanted to play agility with my dog! I rescued a dog at the local shelter, and within a few months, rescued another dog, both to keep the first dog company and so that I could more fully satiate my increasing desire to play the game. There was something highly addicting about spending time with my dogs doing agility.

By the time I went to my second National Event, I was starting to realize that although there were hundreds of fast dogs competing, there were just a few teams that seemed to have a little something 'extra'. This realization didn't make me any more capable of handling myself well under pressure!

I had goals but they were vague and not well defined. I knew what I wanted, but I didn't have any real plan for how to accomplish those things. I also didn't have any real plans for what I would do even if I did accomplish those things. Just running clean three times in a row at Nationals was mentally exhausting for me. My dog was even faster at Nationals than he was at local trials, and keeping it together to make it to the Finals at AKC Nationals took all I had! I knew that I had to do something...something that I was not getting at the gym, or by training more frequently or with more intensity. What I needed was to get control of my mental game.

By the time I made the AKC USA Agility World Team in 2007 with my third dog Jester, I felt like I had control of my mental game. I had spent countless hours reading about, attending seminars about, and practicing strategies to improve my mental performance. I had read just about every sports psychology book ever written. I had made the finals several times with both Jester and Fly, and I had won my first National Championship with Jester. I had won several regional events, and was able to consistently step to the line at those events and have the runs that I envisioned with my dogs.

My big goal for several years had been to make the AKC USA Agility World Team, and in 2007 I did it! I reached my goal! But, despite all my hard work, planning, and short term goal setting,

I had failed to properly address one big piece of the picture; what to do when you reach a major goal.

Reaching your destination can be dangerous if you don't have anything planned for what to do once you GET there! We will explore this issue more in the coming chapters.

Whether your dreams include representing your country at the World Championships, or participating in a local fun match, properly defined goals can help make your dreams a reality. At the end of the day, agility is a game that we play with our dogs, and I believe that becoming skilled at the mental aspects of agility can help both the human and the canine members of the team more fully enjoy the process of training and competing. Goal setting, just like dog training, is a process and a journey, not just a destination.

Clear Mind

Chapter 1
Goal Setting As A Strategy

When asked "why do you participate in agility?" Most of us automatically answer "because it's fun." Of course it is! But what do you want to accomplish? What is your purpose? What is your dream or vision? How do you want to get there? What kind of competitor do you want to be along the way? When you can answer these questions, you are on your way to utilizing goal setting as an intentional strategy for personal success.

Simply stated, our goals are the intended objectives we desire to achieve. Goals define our ambitions and describe what we are working toward. Goals are the reason we work hard in class, train regularly and get up all those early mornings to spend our weekends competing at trials. Goals inspire, encourage and help us persevere when the going gets tough. Goals give our actions direction and provide control. They give our training meaning and offer a sense of value. If done well, our goals also provide a step by step plan on how to achieve success.

By reading this book you are acknowledging the importance of goal setting and the role it can play in your performance and personal success. By the time you complete the activities included in this workbook you will have a solid plan for at least the near future and an understanding of how to set the most effective goals for years to come. You will also learn about who should be involved in helping you set goals and when to modify your goals. By using goal setting training we have seen handlers, who start out unsure of themselves, blossom into confident and consistent handlers, with dogs who follow their lead! *Now* who is having the most fun? This increased self-confidence and sense of efficacy also spreads to other parts of their lives, improving the enjoyment of other activities. Some handlers have even reported that the process actually led to a different way of thinking, changing the way they interpreted their experiences.

"An athlete gains so much knowledge by just participating in a sport. Focus, discipline, hard work, goal setting and, of course, the thrill of finally achieving your goals. These are all lessons in life." Kristi Yamaguchi

What type of handler do you want to be? It is really up to you. Agility handlers who know where they are heading, and have a plan on how to get there, are those who can ride the ups and downs of trialing with character, class, and a sense of humor to boot. They keep the bigger picture in mind and know that each run they take, and each event in which they participate, is a small step in their personal journey. No single run, good or bad, will make or break these handlers. They are the handlers that use their own performance as the yardstick by which to measure satisfaction and success. They view their achievements with pride and their mistakes as opportunities to learn and improve.

While others may simply watch the top handlers, those with a solid goal plan can easily admire another competitor for what they bring to the sport and learn from their observations. After all, they know specifically what they are looking for. These are also the handlers who, rather than waste time blaming their dog, the judge or the weather, will take full responsibility for their experience. They are positive in their approach and supportive of competitors regardless of where they stand in comparison. In the end, they realize agility has the potential to be filled with continuous challenge, reflection, and personal growth.

"Setting a goal is not the main thing. It is deciding how you will go about achieving it and staying with that plan." Tom Landry, Hall of Fame Coach

When taking part in the dynamic process of setting effective goals, several positive changes to the handler's observable behavior, thoughts and cognitive processes, and emotions are often reported. Among these changes is an improvement in our time management. Many of us have limited ability to train, so making the most of what time we have with our dogs in class, or in our back yards, is important. When our path is clearly defined, the time we do commit to training represents an increase in goal directed behavior. It is the quality of our training, not the quantity, which holds great potential to change our performance.

We all know that training and competing can often times feel like one step forward, two steps back, only to be followed by another spring ahead. Identifying overall improvement helps fill us with the determination needed to succeed. This determination translates to

OBSERVABLE

Provides a plan,
time management,
goal directed action,
increased effort &
team building.

COGNITIVE

Improved focus,
attention,
problem solving,
self-awareness &
perceived ability.

EMOTIONAL

Improved self-
efficacy,
confidence &
motivation.

sustained effort, allowing us to work through our weaknesses and make greater advances using our strengths.

Goal setting also produces several cognitive changes including improved focus, accurate self-awareness, and a realistic

perceived ability. If our goal setting includes both short term and long term plans, each time we practice we should have a specific idea regarding what we want to work on. We are able to fine tune the skills we have deemed important to overall improvement, while at the same time ignore aspects that may be less important at a particular time. This deliberate approach to our training allows for an improved self-awareness. With greater self-awareness comes a fuller, more realistic view of our abilities, both our talents and areas that may need work. Several emotional changes have also been associated with goal setting as a training strategy. These include an increase in motivation, a boost in confidence, as well as an increase in feelings of self-efficacy. These feelings of self-belief can assist handlers to take on greater challenge, attempt new ways of handling, or place themselves in situations that have the potential for greater payoffs to their handling proficiency.

When goal setting is implemented in a club or team environment a greater sense of cohesion among members is often observed. The team goals seem to bring members together for a common good and individual aspirations are viewed as stepping stones to the greater collective destination. Apply this concept to your club or training facility and you will be on your way to creating a positive, supportive and healthy environment for your students and staff.

ACTIVITY 1 – KNOWING THE "BIG PICTURE"

 While many handlers may have an idea of what they want to achieve, few use goal setting to its fullest potential - as a strategy to deliberately achieve personal success. Our first exercise is designed to get you started – to start imagining the bigger picture. We will continue with additional exercises included in the chapters that follow to shape these initial ideas into an target plan full of effective goals - goals that will serve as your preliminary foundation on which to build even more future success.

Find a quiet place where you will not be disturbed or interrupted. Close your eyes and try to imagine the time when you will retire your current canine partner from competition.

- What do you want to have achieved together? Is it an award, a title, or perhaps a certain level of competition?
- What kinds of skills do you want to have obtained?
- What types of experiences have you shared?
- How do you want to be remembered by your fellow competitors and club members?

Use the space below to write down your thoughts. The answers may come quickly and you will be ready to move on to the next chapter. For others, it may take a few days of reflection to honestly and completely develop your responses. You do not need to know every detail and, as you will learn in the following chapters, it is also perfectly acceptable to remain flexible. As you work through the remaining exercises in the chapters that follow, you will find that your ideas will take shape more thoroughly.

_____

_____

_____

_____

_____

_____

_____

_____

_____

_____

_____

_____

_____

_____

_____

_____

_____

_____

_____

_____

_____

_____

_____

What do I want to have achieved with my current competition dog at the end of our career together? I would like to have competed at least once at the International level, in particular at the FCI World Agility Championships.

What kinds of skills do I want to have obtained with my current competition dog at the end of our career together? I would like to have achieved the types of skills required to handle International level courses, including the ability to handle my dog's running dogwalk and A-frame.

How do I want to be remembered by my fellow competitors and club members? I feel a deep personal desire to achieve excellence in my performances with my dogs, and I view trophies and ribbons as mementos of excellent performances - when my relationship and team skills with my dog just happened to outshine those of my competitors. But, the real trophy is the relationship I cherish with each of my dogs, and that is what I want to achieve, and how I want to be remembered by my peers.

Getting the initial ideas down on paper for this activity was an important first step in your goal setting journey. However, there is so much more that you can do to make your goals as effective as possible.

Goals should be principle-based. There is no right or wrong goal as long as it is important to you, but there are ways you can plan and define your goals in order to make them as valuable and advantageous to your overall performance as possible. Working through the next few chapters you will start on a targeted plan and learn important goal setting principles. Completing the activities within each chapter will help to create influential, engaging, and beneficial goals. Don't set too many goals to start. A paced and focused approach is the best way to begin, especially if you have not completed a goal setting plan in the past. This will also allow you plenty of space to modify as you improve your self-awareness and performance.

Goal setting will give you an edge – that little something extra that will take your training and handling to an elevated level.

Clear Mind

CHAPTER 2
THE TARGET PLAN

In this chapter we will get started on a method of organizing your training in advance and in relation to the competitive events that you consider to be the most significant. Taking an organized approach to your training by developing a "Target Goal Plan" will allow you to view your aspirations in relation to a specific time line. It will also allow you to readily take a prominent or longer term goal and break it up into more manageable pieces.

Additional activities in the following chapters will help you complete the plan. Once you have completed the plan you will have a map that will direct your training - training that will allow you to feel fully prepared at a specified point in time. The objective is to reach your highest level of performance at the time of your most important events, and to keep the cycle of improvement continuous.

Depending on what point in the season you start your plan, you may find that your target event is a few weeks away or a few months away. Every plan is unique because it is yours alone. If you are not competing in agility events, you may choose a noncompetitive target you would like to achieve with your dog within the next 6 months. Perhaps you will want to enter a fun match or have your dog master a particular obstacle. Whatever your target may be, tying your goal to a time line is a decisive step necessary to solidify your commitment and motivation.

ACTIVITY 2 – MAPPING EVENTS

 On the following pages two example Target Goal Plans have been provided. In reviewing these plans you can see where the planning starts to take shape. Blank charts for your own use are provided in the Planning section of the book starting on page 69. Complete the following steps:

1. Each chart includes a 6 month time line. Use two charts for year long planning.
2. Starting with the current month, in the first column list each month for the period you want to plan. Given this is a work in progress, you may want to use pencil.
3. In the next column list your key event(s) next to the corresponding month. Key events can include a particular trial you want to enter, championship, an invitational event, or even the date by which you want to accomplish a particular challenge. These become your "targets."
4. Describe the goal(s) you have for each event or date marked.

5. Your plan now represents the events that are important to you and their corresponding goal(s). It also represents the time line by which you desire to achieve that goal. At this time do not worry about the phase and steps to success columns, we will visit these in the activities that follow.

6. Self-Check: By achieving the target goals, do you get closer to your overall vision you described in Activity 1? If not, go back and make sure the two are linked in a meaningful way.

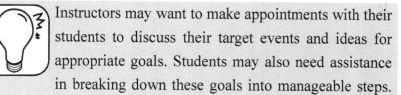 Instructors may want to make appointments with their students to discuss their target events and ideas for appropriate goals. Students may also need assistance in breaking down these goals into manageable steps. This process may also allow instructors to tailor classes or group certain students together to work on specific skills.

Example #1 by Daisy

Month	Target Event & Goal	Phase
Dec		
Jan		
Feb		
Mar	1. AKC Nationals : Make age appropriate course handling decisions for my dog, and concentrate on keeping my timing sharp over multiple runs so that I can provide my young dog a positive experience.	
Apr		
May	2. AKC World Team Tryouts: Make course handling decisions that will highlight the strengths my dog and I possess as a team	

Example #2 Open Level Dog

Month	Target Event & Goal	Phase
Aug	Injury Rehabilitation - to make steady progression in recovery of leg injury while maintaining dog's fitness level	
Sept		
Oct	Return to training class	
Nov	Local trials	
Dec		
Jan	Rose City Classic - to successfully manage my young dog at his first large indoor trial (Crowds, noise, excitement, stimulation and without off-leash areas on site).	

Clear Mind

CHAPTER 3
TRAINING PHASES

With the phenomenal popularity of dog agility and the various competitive formats to choose from, agility has quickly grown to a year round activity. But is competing year round really the most effective strategy? There are many sports that include the option of training and competing on a year round basis. Swimming, tennis, and running are good examples. However, the athletes who are the most successful in these sports do not train at maximal effort on a continual basis. They choose to utilize the strategy of periodization training within their goal plans. The idea is to vary training load over time. Cycling aspects of training has been shown to help athletes avoid over-training and burn-out. In agility you also have your canine partner to think about. Using periodization training will also allow your dog time for recovery and the method helps to avoid boredom and injury.

Early on in my competitive career, I ran agility with my dog nearly every day for at least thirty minutes, and at times up to an hour. That was almost ten years ago, and looking back I can't imagine how either one of us maintained such a rigorous training schedule! Now, my training sessions with my dogs are much shorter, often just a few minutes a few times a week. The difference? I now spend more time *planning* my training sessions before I even take my dogs to the training arena. I also spend more time on physical conditioning for both myself and my dogs. Although I spend less overall time training than I used to, I make more progress with my dogs. Planning breaks from competition during the year helps keep my dogs and I sharp mentally and physically, and, cross-training during those times when we are not doing agility trials, helps prevent injury.

Typically periodization training includes three training phases:
1) preparation phase,
2) competitive phase, and
3) recovery and transition phase.

The *preparation phase* can be thought of as the period of training concerned with skill building. This is the time where you want to identify weaknesses in your handling and take action to strengthen these skills. It is also a time to fine-tune the aspects of handling that you already do well. Learn to use these strong points in ways that could compensate for a weak link in your handling and improve overall performance.

The *competitive phase* is when the skill set is applied within the trial environment. The first cycle does not necessarily include those trials that have been identified as the target event(s). The trials leading up to your target event, serve to accumulate competitive experience as a team that you can draw upon in the future. Cycling through preparation and competition can occur quite frequently depending on your personal goals and choices.

The third phase allows time for *recovery* and then a gradual *transition* into a heavier training load. How many of you have deliberately planned a recovery and transition phase? Rarely does the recovery and transition phase receive the same amount of attention as the preparation and competitive phases despite its importance to the overall health and well-being of the handler and team.

Depending on your time line, recovery can include active rest. This is when you and your dog may participate in other forms of activity such as hiking, herding, or swimming. You can stay physically on the go, but you are varying the environment, skills, and focus used for agility. Transition is your gradual reintroduction to agility training. This is a time that many handlers find useful for reevaluating their goals, and improving their target plan. Transition can be of any duration appropriate to your overall time line but should always avoid sudden changes in activity level.

> *"I never could have achieved the success that I have without setting physical activity and health goals."*
> Bonnie Blair

The following is a general outline of using the periodization training approach. The plan was purposefully described using general statements. Using the activities included in the chapters that follow, these general statements were later shaped into more specific, positive, and performance oriented goals. Can you identify the training phases in this plan?

My yearly cycle typically begins in early or mid-December. From the last National event of the year that I participate in, typically mid-October or early November, until mid-December my dogs and I don't do any agility training at all. Walks or hikes, and some fun trick training, and lots of time spent snuggling on the couch together make up the bulk of our time during those weeks. Beginning in early or mid-December, we start going on hikes that are a little more difficult, and I begin conditioning the dogs more by doing fun tricks on balance disks and balls. I also typically go all the way back to the beginning of the foundation program I use for my dogs' jumping skills. Although they progress through the program more quickly than they did when they were first learning to jump, we always spend some time reviewing the fundamentals at slow speed, so that they are reminded mentally and physically what the demands of the task are.

From January to March, I attend local trials with my dogs. The first few trials are just to get back in to the swing of things and to tune up our teamwork and timing. By the time the end of March arrives, I aim to be physically fit, with well conditioned dogs, and for our teamwork to be strong and well-tuned. My first target event is AKC Nationals, which occurs at the end of March.

After AKC Nationals, I make sure to take a few days to mentally recover from the stresses of traveling and competing at a big event, but I don't cut back on my physical conditioning or that of my dogs. In the month of April we switch gears and focus on refining skills required for international style courses, the type I will expect to see at the beginning of May at World Team Tryouts, my next target event. Any local events during the month of April are used to get in to the mindset of running assertively with my dog without sacrificing attention to detail.

After World Team Tryouts, my dogs and I take a break that typically lasts to mid or late-May. Although we may still be competing at local or regional trials during this time, we are 'competing easy'; not pushing for too much speed, and concentrating on relaxing and regrouping. In June, if I have made the USA AKC World Team with a dog, we are preparing for the next target event, World Championships, which arrives at the end of September!

Activity 3 - Mapping Cycles

 Review your plan started in Activity 2 and within the "Phase" column identify preparation phase(s), competitive phase(s), and recovery/transition phase(s). This should be done with your target events in mind. Again, depending on your personal choices, your target goal plan may include one or more cycles. Two examples have been provided for you, both adding to the examples provided in Activity 2.

EXAMPLE #1 BY DAISY

MONTH	TARGET EVENT & GOAL	PHASE
Dec		Recovery & Transition
		Preparation
Jan		
Feb		
		Competition
Mar	1. AKC Nationals : Make age appropriate course concentrate on keeping my timing sharp over multiple runs so that I can provide my young dog a positive experience.	
Apr		Recovery
		Preparation
May	2. AKC World Team Tryouts: Make course handling decisions that will highlight the strengths my dog and I possess as a team	Competition
		Recovery
		Preparation

EXAMPLE #2 OPEN LEVEL DOG

MONTH	TARGET EVENT & GOAL	PHASE
Aug	Injury Rehabilitation - to make steady progression in recovery of leg injury while maintaining dog's fitness level	Recovery & Transition
Sept		
Oct	Return to training class	
Nov	Return to local trials	Preparation
Dec		
Jan	Rose City Classic - to successfully manage my young dog at his first large indoor trial (crowds, noise, excitement, stimulation and no off-leash areas on site).	Competition

CHAPTER 4
PERFORMANCE AND OUTCOMES

Understanding the key differences between performance and outcome goals, and learning to integrate both into your goals setting plan, is perhaps the most important principle to master. Performance goals are those that focus on actions and skills necessary to improve handling ability. These are the task-oriented goals – the tools in your toolbox. They identify particular aspects or skills that will take your handling to the next level. By focusing on particular skills, we find that handlers become more intrinsically motivated, define standards by their own performance, and look for ways to personally challenge themselves.

In comparison, outcome goals are aspects of the sport that usually take place following our performance. These include external rewards such as placements, ribbons, trophies, points, team memberships or prize money. Unfortunately, these goals may not be consistently related to the quality of our performance or the depth of our skill set. A common outcome goal among athletes is "I want to win." While there is nothing wrong with wanting to win or even

> *"The will to win is important, but the will to prepare to win is vital."* Joe Paterno

wanting to be the "best," outcome goals should not be our focus while we are on the course with our dog.

Outcome goals are sometimes referred to in the research literature as ego-oriented goals as they often result in social comparison as a way to define self-worth. The problem comes when a handler becomes over reliant on outcomes to define their success or proficiency in the sport rather than on individual progress and achievement of particular skills. It is a precarious place to be. No matter who we are or how good we may be, we simply cannot win every event or even be the best at all times. Extreme dependence on outcomes can soon lead to a loss of skill development, motivation, and confidence.

When contemplating performance and outcome goals, we quickly come to the conclusion that both are a fundamental part of any competitive sport, and agility is no exception. The entire system of each agility organization is structured around the pursuit of outcomes. Qualifying runs determine titles and advancements to higher levels of competition. Placements and competition points determine who is chosen for various teams or invitational events. Nevertheless, being wrapped up with thoughts of the outcomes only distract from the immediate task, the demands of the course.

> *"Spectacular achievements are always preceded by unspectacular preparation."* Roger Staubach, Hall of Fame Football Player

So how do we unite the two concepts of both performance and outcomes in a healthy, productive manner? The answer begins with utilizing performance goals as a means to define and develop a required skill set - maximizing our knowledge base within the physical, technical, tactical and mental aspects of the sport. This process is followed by the practice of applying the achieved skill set in class, a competitive situation, or under times of pressure, in order to produce a desired outcome. The approach relies heavily on skill building, while still recognizing the importance of the outcome. When your skill set meets or exceeds a given set of demands, the outcomes will take care of themselves.

> *"Winning is the science of being totally prepared."*
> *George Allen, Hall of Fame Football Coach*

PERFORMANCE GOALS
Building skill set to maximize abilities in the physical, technical, tactical and mental aspects of the sport.

OUTCOME GOALS
Application of skill set in order to meet or exceed the demands of the sport, thereby producing the desired outcome.

While competing with Solar at the 2010 World Agility Championships in Germany, I had an experience I will never forget, one that will forever remind me to maintain an attitude that supports the achievement of performance goals rather than outcome oriented goals.

I had two runs at World Championships, a Jumpers With Weaves run and a Standard run. My JWW run was first, and although my randomly assigned run order number was five, three of the people ahead of me did not run, and so I was second to run. I felt over stimulated and was consumed with thoughts of doing everything right. My run was clean, but disconnected, and I came in 31st. I was not happy at all with my run. Not only did the outcome reflect my lack of attention to my performance, but I was so nervous I couldn't even remember the run very well. Therefore I was left with no opportunity to enjoy or relive that moment with my dog at his first International event.

By the time the STD run came the following day, I was determined to have a different experience. Of course, I wanted another clean run, but more importantly, I wanted to have a run with my dog where I felt connected and present; a run that both of us could remember. Before stepping to the line, I looked down at my dog and my eyes filled with tears. I was so proud of the both of us. Fully committed to enjoying every moment, I waved to the crowd as Solar and I were announced. As I led out to my start position I had a clear image of the course and what I wanted to do. The result was a run that will forever be imprinted on my mind. I didn't need to check the scoreboard to know how well we had

done. I was so proud of the two of us during that run that nothing else mattered.

Twenty minutes later when I finished cooling Solar down I headed back to the stands. Our STD results had put us in first place overall, and we stayed at the top until nearly the very end, eventually dropping to 6th place. This amazing finish was a reflection of my focus on performance and not on any particular outcome.

ACTIVITY 4 – USING PERFORMANCE GOALS AS STEPS TO SUCCESS

Refer back to your target goal plan. For each training phase you have identified, create at least one performance goal and describe it in the column labeled "Steps to Success." Be sure to create goals that are related to your overall mission from Activity 1, your target events and goals in Activity 2, and to the specific training phases you have planned in Activity 3. In the end you should have a series of performance goals that are directly linked to the desired outcome. You have now described a focus for each phase of training leading up to your target event(s) or date(s). Two examples carried forward from the previous activities are included for your review.

EXAMPLE #1 BY DAISY

MONTH	TARGET EVENT & GOAL	PHASE
Dec		Recovery & Transition
		Preparation
Jan		
Feb		
		Competition
Mar	1. AKC Nationals : Make age appropriate course concentrate on keeping my timing sharp over multiple runs so that I can provide my young dog a positive experience.	
Apr		Recovery
		Preparation
May	2. AKC World Team Tryouts: Make course handling decisions that will highlight the strengths my dog and I possess as a team	Competition
		Recovery
		Preparation

Clear Mind

STEPS TO SUCCESS

Two hikes per week and short walk each day. Reestablish communication with personal trainer. Increase amount of physio-ball work with dogs to 3x/week.

Enter trials being mindful of where we are as a team. Make note of any weaknesses. Continue hiking and physio work, as well as foundation jump training. Session with personal trainer 2x/week, work out either at home or gym 3 additional sessions/week.

As Preparation phase draws nearer to competition (February), focus on competing to the strengths of the team (make tactical decisions on course that support strengths and avoid depending on weaknesses).

Keep up with physical conditioning for dog, 2-3 hikes/week, 3-5 physio-ball sessions/week, 2 sessions/week with personal trainer, increased intensity at gym/home workouts. Increased focus on sprinting and quick acceleration/deceleration. Evaluate and adjust nutrition for dog and myself as needed to maintain condition during travel.

At local competitions, step to line with the attitude "this is it." Put pressure on myself to do well in preparation for a big event, where the performance is particularly important to achieving the outcome.

Maintain physical fitness but take short break from agility. Continue with hikes and personal trainer.

Study courses by international judges. Set up sequences/courses based on international challenges. Address foundation skills needed to support successful completion of these challenges.

Focus on process only - trust our conditioning and training. Evaluate all possible course handling strategies and pick those that depend on our known strengths.

Full break from training (3 wks). Easy hikes/walks only.

Carefully increase levels of hikes and training. Compete "easy."

EXAMPLE #2 OPEN LEVEL DOG

Month	Target Event & Goal	Phase
Aug	Injury Rehabilitation - to make steady progression in my own recovery of leg injury while maintaining dog's fitness level	Recovery & Transition
Sept		
Oct	Return to training class	
Nov	Return to local trials	Preparation
Dec		
Jan	Rose City Classic - to successfully manage my young dog at his first large indoor trial (crowds, noise, excitement, stimulation and without off-leash areas on site).	Competition

STEPS TO SUCCESS

2 weeks complete rest (no weight bearing).
Dog - kids to take dog to park (frisbee, ball, sprints)

Light walking. Focus on warm-up and post-walk stretching.
P/T 2x per week.

Dog - foundation jump work, weaves, table, A-frame.
Continue park sessions with kids.

Short runs and sprints with dog as permitted by P/T.

Research footwear for different surfaces.

Increase run times as permitted.

Deliberate warm-ups, cool-down and stretching in class.

Enter single day trial to evaluate leg after run. Goal is to keep pace with dog.

Order new footwear.

Increase runs to include sprints 3x week.

Enter 2 day trials. Focus on working as a team and keeping pace with dog during run. Lots of eye contact.
Deliberate warm-up, cool-down and stretching during trial.

Arrive a day early. Kennel placement in low traffic area. Walk grounds and ring area with dog. Locate pre-trial exercise area that we can use prior to arriving at trial in mornings. Reinforce appropriate behavior often and consistently throughout the day, both in and out of kennel. Create positive experience for dog with short kennel stays and frequent breaks outside.

CHAPTER 5
WITHIN YOUR CONTROL

Within any sport or activity there are elements which we can and cannot control. Handlers who choose goals that rely on elements of the sport that are within their control can gain satisfaction in any environment, and accomplishment can be identified on a continual basis. While we cannot always control what happens to us or our dog, we can control how we respond. We can control our attitude, emotions, how hard we work, and how frequently we train. We can also control what we train and where we choose to train. By allowing these controllable aspects of our handling to become the essential elements of our goals, success lies within our own power.

There are aspects of agility over which we have no control and our goals should not be dependent on these. If we ignore this idea, we give up our power to direct our own success. A few of the elements of agility that are outside of our control include course design, judging, equipment at a trial, surface type or weather conditions. So what can we do to respond to these uncontrollable aspects? We can train to minimize the impact that these elements have on our performance. For example, each agility organization has a set of rules and regulations used for designing courses. Be aware of the particular challenges that each type of course may present and incorporate this knowledge into your training sessions. Save your course maps and make notes after running to refer to after the trial. Did you experience any challenges? Set up these portions of the course to refine or improve your handling.

"What has benefited me the most is learning I can't control what happens outside of my pitching."
Greg Maddox

Not all elements are clearly outside of our control or within our control. For example, there is no dog agility without the dog, so where do you place your dog along the dimension of controllability? Isn't the entire reason we train to move our dog's behavior from uncontrollable to as controllable as possible? Is it possible to have an animal fully under our control, under all circumstances? I am sure your answer depends on your experience, expertise, and environment - and of course, your dog. The debate about the controllability of each handler's dog is an interesting topic of conversation to initiate among a group. The realization that we all face moving our dogs to the controllable side of the equation should help in supporting one another along this journey.

"This ability to conquer oneself is no doubt the most precious of all things sports bestows." Olga Korbut

Most of us would consider an injury an uncontrollable event. Injury is undesirable and it is unplanned. To reduce the risk of injury, in both ourselves and our dogs, we can take part in proper and deliberate physical training. With a sport specific fitness regimen we can strengthen the muscles, joints and movements needed for the quick turns, sprints, and acceleration required to perform well on a course. While being in better condition does not eliminate the risk of injury, it does reduce the occurrence of injuries and can speed up recovery time. Consequently, controlling our fitness level helps to control the impact of an injury.

Let's examine the weather as another example. In Sumner, WA we are lucky to have indoor training year round. But this is not necessarily an advantage when we find ourselves at a rainy outdoor trial. Our dog's footing is not as precise on wet grass and our own timing with our dog is also altered. Of course the weather and the wet grass are outside of our control. However, we can plan to spend time training outside in the rain to gain knowledge and experience in that

"Failing to prepare is preparing to fail." Wayne Gretzky

situation. By learning how our dog's timing may change on the wet grass, and making appropriate adjustments to our own handling, we should find ourselves more prepared at the next rainy trial.

Two common pursuits in the sport of agility are; 1) gaining qualifying runs or Q'ing, and 2) winning or placing. Both are important outcome goals and both are required for advancement. However, with regard to controllability, they are also quite different from one another.

Qualifying can be defined as:
    a) applying a required set of skills to
    b) meet the demands of a specific course, while
    c) following a specific set of rules for that particular event,
    d) during a trial or within a competitive situation.

All four components of this definition can be incorporated into our performance goals. While we do not know ahead of time the demands of the course we may face at a trial, we can train for a variety of demands to increase our odds of having the experience and skills necessary to handle the course proficiently. We can also ensure we know the set of rules by reading the appropriate information prior to the event. Our overall knowledge of the trial situation is improved each time we compete, and our experience within the competitive environment grows. Q'ing therefore moves closer to a controllable event over time.

Winning or placing is similar to qualifying because it is also an outcome

"I concentrate on preparing to swim my race and let the other swimmers think about me, not me about them."
Amanda Beard

goal, but with one critical difference. The outcome depends on who we may be running against during a particular event, on a specific day. Handlers whose goal depends on defeating others, or whose definition of success is winning, are not in control. These types of goals depend heavily on the performance of the other handlers - how they perform during a given run, compared to how we ourselves perform. Over time, those who focus on the defeat of others take less risk and may avoid challenging themselves altogether for fear they may fail.

ACTIVITY 5 – CHARTING ASPECTS OF AGILITY

Take a moment to evaluate the aspects of agility with respect to the dimension of controllability. A chart has been provided for you on the next page with a few ideas to get you started. Once complete, review your target goal plan and determine if any of the goals you have described rely on aspects outside your control. If so, adjust your goal so that you are in complete command over whether or not you have the ability to achieve the goal. Develop additional goals to help reduce the impact of those outside of your control and add these to your target goal plan. This activity can also be a great group project. Completing the chart with another handler, your team, or class can be a lot of fun and result in meaningful discussion.

CHARTING ASPECTS OF AGILITY WITHIN AND OUTSIDE OF HANDLER'S CONTROL

CONTROLLABLE	UNCONTROLLABLE
Training schedules Trial schedule Diet / Nutrition / Fitness	Weather Course Design Judging Attitude of other competitors Ability of other competitors Equipment in use at a trial

CHAPTER 6
THE LANGUAGE OF GOAL SETTING

W hat to do or what *not* to do? No, this is not Shakespeare, but it is a question we should contemplate. What side of the question do you normally think about? Should our goals be about the things we want to avoid or should they be about the effect we want to achieve? The answer is our goals should be stated in the positive rather than the negative. This principle is simply about the language of goal setting. You will be amazed at how putting this principle into action will change your outlook.

Identify behaviors you want to strive toward, rather than behaviors you want to avoid. State what you want to achieve, using positive determined language. How many of us have heard things like "I don't want to miss the contact," "I don't want my dog to break the start line," or "I don't want a fly-off." Start listening to conversations around you at an agility trial and you will likely hear what people don't want to have happen and perhaps less about what they actually want to accomplish.

Teaching a dog to walk on a leash is an easy example of how to change a goal from the negative to the positive. Many dog owners will start by saying "I don't want my dog to pull on his leash." Well that is great – we completely agree – but this is only stating the problem,

"Success depends less on strength of body than upon strength of mind and character."
Arnold Palmer

describing what they want to avoid. We are left with a variety of options for a solution. Does this owner want the dog to walk off-leash? Learn to ride a skateboard? What about those people you see pushing their dogs around in a cart? Is this what they had in mind? More likely they want to be able to walk with their dog beside them, happily trotting along, the leash dangling loosely between them. Not having said what they would like, we are left only to assume what the actual intention may be.

"A man who views the world the same at fifty as he did at twenty has wasted thirty years of his life."Muhammad Ali

A pattern we commonly hear while at trials is "I don't want [fill in the blank]…" For example, "I don't want my dog to get ahead of me." Again, we can all agree. Letting our dog get ahead and knowing the judge's arm just shot in the air because he just went off course is not a pleasing experience. But the negative statement doesn't do us much good when deciding our course strategy. Have you ever voiced what you want to steer clear of? Most of us have. Next time

  Clear Mind

try catching yourself and turn it around. We need to determine what needs to be done in order to give ourselves, and our dog, the best chance possible to work as a team on the course and stay together. In this example, we can walk the course, head turned back over our shoulder, as though our dog is behind us. We can visualize what it looks like and how it feels to be ahead and determine where we will need to be relative to our dog. Our goal is to be at the determined location on the course at the right time. This is a performance goal, which is within our control, stated using affirmative language. We have in fact shifted our attention to the ideal situation.

This approach may take some getting used to but try to describe the desired action rather than the undesirable. Be your own leader by letting your goals describe your path.

Activity 6 – Re-framing: Stating the Positive

1) Review the goals you listed on your target goal plan and determine if any are stated using negative language. Take any negative goals you may find and transform them using positive language. 2) Think about your recent training. Can you identify any persistent problems? Take these "problems" and describe your solution.

Make sure you are describing the desired behavior rather than a behavior you want to avoid.

Negative (Problem)	Positive (Solution)

Clear Mind

CHAPTER 7
DIFFICULT YET REALISTIC GOALS

The goals we set for ourselves should be challenging but we should also possess the potential to achieve these challenging goals. In order to set difficult yet realistic goals we must all start with an honest self-evaluation of our current ability level and our potential to improve. Whether you are new to the sport or a seasoned veteran you may want to turn to your instructor, team or other trusted agility friend to help with your self-assessment. This may be one of the most difficult phases of goal setting but it is well worth the discomfort.

We should also include an evaluation of our dog's ability and drive. If you desire the top level of competition but your dog does not have the structure or drive to train at this level, you set yourself up for disappointment or frustration instead of success. If you can only devote an hour a week but your dog is high drive and in need of consistent stimuli, perhaps you need to think about adding a few back yard sessions or additional activities to your routine. We all need to remember this is a team sport in which both handler and dog need to be taken into consideration when choosing goals.

"The quality of a person's life is in direct proportion to their commitment to excellence, regardless of their chosen field."
Vince Lombardi

We also need to realistically evaluate our availability to train, the quality of that training, and the resources we have access to. If you can devote a consistent number of high quality sessions per week your goals have the potential to be more demanding or progress at a faster rate than if you complete an inconsistent number of unplanned training sessions every couple of weeks. A similar evaluation of your

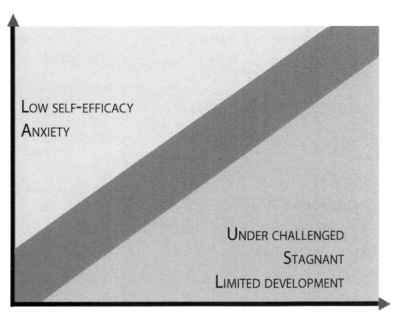

LEVEL OF DIFFICULTY / DEMANDS

LOW SELF-EFFICACY
ANXIETY

UNDER CHALLENGED
STAGNANT
LIMITED DEVELOPMENT

SKILL SET / RESOURCES

  Clear Mind

existing resources should also be included. Have you considered your budget for entering trials, travel, and instruction? Do you have the opportunity to gain knowledge through other sources of information such as books, tapes, video or seminars? How accessible is your training facility or practice equipment? How much planning are you willing to devote so that your training is the highest quality and makes the best use of your time?

Setting realistic goals is about balancing the level of difficulty of your goals with your skill set and resources. In the chart below we want to achieve the balance represented within the dark band. This is where our goals meet or moderately exceed our skills, training and experience. This is where we feel challenged but not overwhelmed. When training and competing in this zone, development as a handler occurs at a reasonable pace, with consistent tests and continual learning. Confidence and self-reliance follow accordingly.

If we set our goals with demands and difficulty levels that far exceed our skill set and potential we have set ourselves up for disappointment and frustration (top left of the chart). These types of goals will need adjustment so that we do not place ourselves in situations for which we are simply not yet ready. Too much time in this position can produce problems such as low self-efficacy and issues relating to anxiety.

The bottom right of the chart represents when our goals are far below what we are capable of. We find ourselves under challenged, perhaps even bored. Development of skills is limited or non-existent. When left in this position too long we end up feeling stagnant. Goals that hold more demand are needed in order for growth to occur.

Activity 7 – Self Assessment

 Arrange for a meeting with your instructor, teammate or other trusted agility friend who has knowledge about your current level of performance and who will provide honest and supportive feedback regarding your potential to improve. Together, review the consultation questions below with regard to the goals you have identified in the previous exercises.

1. Is it realistic for me to have this as my goal?
2. Will this goal be a challenge?
3. Do I have the physical and psychological potential?
4. Does my dog have the physical and psychological potential?
5. Do I have adequate opportunity and resources available to achieve this goal?
6. What is the commitment necessary to achieve this goal?
7. Am I willing to exert the amount of effort that is needed?
8. Is this goal a performance or outcome goal?
9. If it is an outcome goal, what are the elements of performance I will need to develop to produce the outcome?
10. What are some of the smaller steps I can take toward the larger goal?
11. Have I stated this goal positively?
12. Is this goal within my control?
13. What are some potential obstacles I may encounter in striving to achieve this goal?
14. What are the planned solutions to these obstacles?

CHAPTER 8
SPECIFIC MEASURABLE GOALS

S etting specific goals is the measurable, sequential process to achieving greater results over time. The more specific we can state our goals the more effective they will be in influencing change. We should be able to clearly measure and accurately monitor our progress toward our goals using specific criteria. There should be no question in our minds how close we are to achieving our goals. We also should be able to easily recognize improvement and identify strengths and weaknesses, as it directly relates to the goals we set out to achieve.

For example, we all want to be a "good handler" or even a "better handler" but what does this really mean? This goal is far too general to be meaningful. Each handler will have a unique and personal definition of what it means to them to be "good" or "better." It is this definition that will ultimately lead to individual goals that are separate and tailored to each dog-handler team. Even for the same handler, the goals may be very different depending on what dog they may be teamed with. While the big picture, or in this case the general goal, is a good starting point, it is the specific details of the goal setting plan that will initiate change. Moving from the general to the specific will help shape training and focus.

"It is better to look ahead and prepare than to look back and regret." Jackie Joyner-Kersee

For example, a handler noticed that her dog's A-frame needed improving. Using specific and measurable goals she set out to decrease the time it took her dog to complete the A-frame. She set the electronic start and finish timers at either end of the A-frame, then calculated her dog's average time over 5 runs. This provided her with a basis from which to improve her "before" level of performance. Knowing this baseline allowed her to accurately note how differences in approach and release changed her dog's performance.

Another example was when a handler had an issue with her dog stopping short at the end of the dog walk. She desired a consistent 2-on 2-off execution. She began by measuring a rate of correct performance as a percentage of attempts. This provided a base from which to track improvement. Her training goals became focused on the performance at end of the dog walk and a plan was made to re-

"Our goals can only be reached through a vehicle of a plan, in which we must fervently believe, and upon which we must vigorously act. There is no other route to success." Stephen A. Brennan

measure in a few weeks. The measurable rate of correct performance will give her an indication of progress toward her consistent 2-on 2-off goal.

At times the goal may be applicable to only the handler. For instance, a handler was having trouble keeping in front of her dog, especially as he matured and grew stronger. Several times this caused errors on course and left the team frustrated at the end of trial weekends. Working with her instructor they moved from a general improvement approach to a specific goal. She found that in order to correct the situation she needed to improve her strength and sprinting speed. The example is sketched out below.

To be a better handler

To be capable of getting in front of my dog when needed.

To improve my sprinting ability

Reduce my average 50m time from 10sec to 8sec

ACTIVITY 8 – NARROWING YOUR OBJECTIVES

 Keeping the approach described above in mind, read over your target events and related goal(s). Review the training phases you have identified on your target goal plan, and the corresponding "Steps to Success." From Steps to Success you may need to get even more specific, much like we did in the previous sketch. Space has been provided on the following pages for you to sketch out your own plan. These more specific goals are natural steps toward the larger more distant goals. Incorporating both the short and long term goals provides the purposeful practical plan needed for personal success.

_____

_____

_____

_____

_____

_____

_____

_____

_____

_____

_____

Clear Mind

CHAPTER 9
GOAL SETTING AS A DYNAMIC PROCESS

Goal setting is not a perfect science and every athlete should view goal setting as a dynamic process. Continual adjustments and modifications to the original plan is a normal part of the goal setting process. Your goals should evolve with experience and achievement, as well as insight and learning. When you meet your goal, excitement, pride, and confidence should follow. These positive attributes should then help lead you to further challenges, growth, and progress. Where one goal leaves off, another should begin.

 By the time I got my third dog, in 2003, I had been doing agility for five years, and knew I wanted to be on the World Team. Everything I did was within the framework of 'making the team'. My dog's training, the hours at the gym, what I ate, even the colors of the leashes I bought, were all done with an intense passion and desire to make the team. I looked and felt better than I ever had in my life; certainly I was more physically fit than I'd ever been!

In 2007, when Jester was just over three years old we won the AKC National Championships. Just over a month later, we were chosen for the 2007 AKC USA World Team, scheduled to compete in Hamar, Norway in the Fall of 2007. Life continued on as usual, which meant I worked out at the gym ceaselessly, and every minute spent training was for World Championships.

However, almost immediately after arriving at World Championships I ran in to a serious problem. Everything I did prior to World Championships was in preparation for getting to that event, and once at the event, there was no further need to engage in any of those behaviors. I felt as though I had been set adrift, with little purpose and no concrete goals. Although mental management experts and even my fellow teammates had warned me of this, I didn't adequately plan for what to do at World Championships, or afterward either. As a consequence my enjoyment as well as my performances suffered dramatically.

As of this writing I have competed for a second time at a World Agility Championship, with another dog, Solar, who is now also a three time National Champion. This time around I have been far more careful to place myself in a situation where I am already looking forward to the next goal. I have taken the time to evaluate how completion of my current goal supports the process of reaching future goals.

One of my goals is to help others overcome similar challenges that I have overcome, and to master their own mental game; hence this workbook!

This story illustrates what can happen when we do not approach goal setting as a dynamic process. The training was obviously well planned, every action had a deliberate purpose and the ultimate goal was reached. However, planning for what would happen after making the team was not in place. The goals simply stopped. Left unprepared for the next step, there was no time to adapt to the increased demands and expectations of international level competition.

A lack of follow-up and evaluation of goal directed behavior is one of the main factors in the failure of a goal setting program.

Athletes need to take the time to close the feedback loop by identifying strengths as well as areas for growth. Using this information to revise and update the goal plan is critical to continued success.

Adjusting your goal plan upward is a natural step that reflects learning and skill improvement. Extending your target goal plan, or even resetting the goal standards, on a regular basis is important for continued improvement and for reminding us of the big picture and what we have to look forward to. The idea of goal setting as a continual process will allow your target goal plan to rejuvenate and recharge.

To succeed in baseball, as in life, you must make adjustments."
Ken Griffey Jr.

The dynamic process of goal setting includes evaluating your experiences, identifying the good along with opportunities for improvement, revising your goal plan accordingly and initiating renewed goal directed behavior. Some handlers find it useful to go through this process after each trial, each month, or during a specified phase of training. You can also leave it flexible and be willing to adapt whenever necessary. It depends on your schedule, opportunity, and goals.

Just as you may need to modify your target goal plan based on your achievements, you may also need to revise based on lack of progress or any obstacles you may encounter. Let's face it. Not everything goes as planned at all times. Modification of your goal plan may be necessary in response to injury, or other unexpected set-backs. This can prove to be very difficult for any athlete. Rather than seeing this type of adjustment as a failure to succeed it should be accepted as a normal part of the goal setting process. Every serious athlete out there has had to adjust their plan at some time. Modifications could be necessary in response to a variety of issues. Even new equipment, or in our case, perhaps a new canine partner, can result in an adjustment.

A thorough analysis of both what worked and what did not work can provide critical information. Making the effort to learn from your mistakes, rather than dwell on them, will help reduce or even eliminate them in the future. When you experience a problem, do you give up? Of course not – you find a solution. Turn your experience into simple, determined, but goal directed decisions. Do not let your experiences go to waste. Whether it is positive or negative, all experience provides information. Teaching moments come in all shapes and sizes. Information gained only adds to your personal expertise and fuels future change.

ACTIVITY 9 – ACTIVE GOAL TRACKING

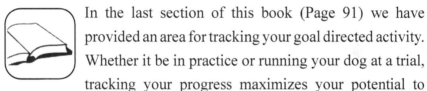 In the last section of this book (Page 91) we have provided an area for tracking your goal directed activity. Whether it be in practice or running your dog at a trial, tracking your progress maximizes your potential to build on experience. Tracking your goal directed activity provides critical feedback necessary for learning and improvement to occur. Noting details such as running surface, weather, or obstacle set-up, in relation to your performance and obtained outcome will provide the information you need to set new goals and keep the dynamic process going. Over time you should become aware of how internal and external factors relate to how you perform, both as a handler and as a team. The key is to keep what you like and improve on what you

don't. Your "tool box" will become bigger and bigger, allowing you to respond successfully in more and more situations.

Don't be shy. Take note of skill improvements and increased consistency. Welcome change and view each run with your dog as an opportunity to learn, grow, and improve. Make adjustments accordingly and enjoy the journey.

CHAPTER 10
FINAL THOUGHTS

We each have our own reasons for participating in agility. For some, agility could be described as recreation, providing a pleasant diversion from work schedules. For others, agility satisfies the need for personal challenge in a competitive sport environment. For all of us, it is a chance to get out and socialize with other like-minded dog lovers and hopefully support one another as we each strive toward our own objectives.

In this fast growing sport of agility our schedules can quickly become consumed with classes, seminars, travel and trials. This is a choice each one of us makes in pursuit of our personal ambitions. Creating a personal target goal plan that includes periodization training and focuses on our target events tied to a specified time-line will serve to remind us of the big picture. No one achievement or single struggle should define us as handlers nor determine our final destination. Rather, each step we take is part of a large continual process of growth and development. When problems do occur we can identify new solutions, and when we evaluate the outcome of our goal directed behavior we have the opportunity to persevere toward making new ideas our next reality.

Goals can be set in a variety of areas. Although this book mainly dealt with individual skill required to be an agility handler, it is important to mention that goals can also be described in the areas of psychological skills, fitness, balancing the demands of family and sport, as well as team and club related goals.

> *"My competitors are not adversaries - they are helpers. They help me push past my limits."*
> *Victor Plata*

Having learned the principles of effective goals setting, we will be sure to set goals that are positive, within our control, and specific. We will use performance tasks to construct our skill set and then apply that set of skills to produce the outcomes we desire. A higher level of self-acceptance and sense of confidence that can carry over to other areas of our daily lives will follow. Goal setting within clubs and teams will provide a sense of collective effort. Members of these clubs and teams will become models of strong competitive drive coupled with solid character. These are the clubs, teams, and individual competitors that others will aspire to be.

> *"When the game is over I just want to look at myself in the mirror, win or lose, and know I gave it everything I had."*
> *Joe Montana*

Agility, like many sports, is filled with ups and downs, positives and negatives, celebrations and disappointment. By choosing to participate we expose both our strengths and our weaknesses, and our challenges make us stronger. Accept the joy of simply running with our dogs and each run can become an opportunity.

While at first working through the process of goal setting may feel time consuming, the more we incorporate the principles into our training the easier the process will become. Over time the process will become a way of thinking, intrinsic to our approach, and will help define us as a competitor. It is our hope that the information contained in this workbook contributes, at least in some small way, to your enjoyment of our incredible sport.

Clear Mind

TARGET GOAL PLANNING CHARTS

DOG:

MONTH	TARGET EVENT & GOAL	PHASE

Clear Mind

STEPS TO SUCCESS

Dog:

Month	Target Event & Goal	Phase

Clear Mind

STEPS TO SUCCESS

Dog:

Month	Target Event & Goal	Phase

Clear Mind

STEPS TO SUCCESS

Dog:

Month	Target Event & Goal	Phase

STEPS TO SUCCESS

Dog:

Month	Target Event & Goal	Phase

STEPS TO SUCCESS

Dog:

Month	Target Event & Goal	Phase

Clear Mind

STEPS TO SUCCESS

Dog:

Month	Target Event & Goal	Phase

Clear Mind

STEPS TO SUCCESS

Dog:

Month	Target Event & Goal	Phase

Clear Mind

Steps to Success

Dog:

Month	Target Event & Goal	Phase

Clear Mind

STEPS TO SUCCESS

Dog:

Month	Target Event & Goal	Phase

Clear Mind

STEPS TO SUCCESS

Clear Mind

GOAL DIRECTED ACTIVITY TRACKING CHARTS

Event	Date
Location	Time
Weather	Surface
Judge/Instructor	Dog

Performance Goal

Extent Achieved: 0 1 2 3 4 5 6 7 8 9 10

Challenge

Performance Strategy

Effectiveness: 0 1 2 3 4 5 6 7 8 9 10

SCT	YDS	Q/NQ	Place
Time	YPS	Points	Title

Notes

Clear Mind

Positive   Specific   Challenging   Within Your Control

What did I like? What do I want to keep for next time?

What do I want to find a solution for? Areas to change or improve?

New or Modified Performance Goal

Performance Dynamic Within Your Control Challenging Specific Positive

Positive Specific Challenging Within Your Control Dynamic Performance

Event	Date
Location	Time
Weather	Surface
Judge/Instructor	Dog

Performance Goal

Extent Achieved: 0 1 2 3 4 5 6 7 8 9 10

Challenge

Performance Strategy

Effectiveness: 0 1 2 3 4 5 6 7 8 9 10

SCT	YDS	Q/NQ	Place
Time	YPS	Points	Title

Notes			

Positive Specific Challenging Within Your Control

Clear Mind

Positive   Specific   Challenging   Within Your Control

What did I like? What do I want to keep for next time?

What do I want to find a solution for? Areas to change or improve?

New or Modified Performance Goal

Performance | Dynamic | Within Your Control | Challenging | Specific | Positive

Event	Date
Location	Time
Weather	Surface
Judge/Instructor	Dog

Performance Goal

Extent Achieved: 0 1 2 3 4 5 6 7 8 9 10

Challenge

Performance Strategy

Effectiveness: 0 1 2 3 4 5 6 7 8 9 10

SCT	YDS	Q/NQ	Place
Time	YPS	Points	Title

Notes

Positive | Specific | Challenging | Within Your Control | Dynamic | Performance

 Clear Mind

Positive

Specific

Challenging

Within Your Control

Dynamic

Performance

What did I like? What do I want to keep for next time?

Within Your Control

Challenging

What do I want to find a solution for? Areas to change or improve?

Dynamic

Performance

Specific

New or Modified Performance Goal

Positive

Positive
Specific
Challenging
Within Your Control
Dynamic
Performance

Performance

Dynamic

Within Your Control

Challenging

Specific

Positive

Event		Date	
Location		Time	
Weather		Surface	
Judge/Instructor		Dog	

Performance Goal

Extent Achieved: 0 1 2 3 4 5 6 7 8 9 10

Challenge

Performance Strategy

Effectiveness: 0 1 2 3 4 5 6 7 8 9 10

SCT	YDS	Q/NQ	Place
Time	YPS	Points	Title

Notes

 Clear Mind

Positive   Specific   Challenging   Within Your Control

What did I like? What do I want to keep for next time?

What do I want to find a solution for? Areas to change or improve?

New or Modified Performance Goal

Event		Date	
Location		Time	
Weather		Surface	
Judge/Instructor		Dog	

Performance Goal

Extent Achieved: 0 1 2 3 4 5 6 7 8 9 10

Challenge

Performance Strategy

Effectiveness: 0 1 2 3 4 5 6 7 8 9 10

SCT	YDS	Q/NQ	Place
Time	YPS	Points	Title

Notes			

Clear Mind

Positive   Specific   Challenging   Within Your Control

What did I like? What do I want to keep for next time?	
What do I want to find a solution for? Areas to change or improve?	
New or Modified Performance Goal	

(Margin labels, left side, bottom to top): Positive Specific Challenging Within Your Control Dynamic Performance

(Margin labels, right side, top to bottom): Positive Specific Challenging Within Your Control Dynamic Performance

(Margin labels, bottom, right to left): Positive Specific Challenging Within Your Control

Performance   Dynamic   Within Your Control   Challenging   Specific   Positive

Event	Date
Location	Time
Weather	Surface
Judge/Instructor	Dog

Performance Goal

Extent Achieved: 0   1   2   3   4   5   6   7   8   9   10

Challenge

Performance Strategy

Effectiveness: 0   1   2   3   4   5   6   7   8   9   10

SCT	YDS	Q/NQ	Place
Time	YPS	Points	Title
Notes			

Positive   Specific   Challenging   Within Your Control   Dynamic   Performance

Positive   Specific   Challenging   Within Your Control

What did I like? What do I want to keep for next time?	
What do I want to find a solution for? Areas to change or improve?	
New or Modified Performance Goal	

Event	Date
Location	Time
Weather	Surface
Judge/Instructor	Dog

Performance Goal

Extent Achieved: 0 1 2 3 4 5 6 7 8 9 10

Challenge

Performance Strategy

Effectiveness: 0 1 2 3 4 5 6 7 8 9 10

SCT	YDS	Q/NQ	Place
Time	YPS	Points	Title

Notes

104   Clear Mind

Positive   Specific   Challenging   Within Your Control

What did I like? What do I want to keep for next time?

What do I want to find a solution for? Areas to change or improve?

New or Modified Performance Goal

Performance   Dynamic   Within Your Control   Challenging   Specific   Positive

Positive   Specific   Challenging   Within Your Control   Dynamic   Performance

Event	Date
Location	Time
Weather	Surface
Judge/Instructor	Dog

Performance Goal

Extent Achieved: 0 1 2 3 4 5 6 7 8 9 10

Challenge

Performance Strategy

Effectiveness: 0 1 2 3 4 5 6 7 8 9 10

SCT	YDS	Q/NQ	Place
Time	YPS	Points	Title

Notes

Clear Mind

Positive   Specific   Challenging   Within Your Control

Positive	
Specific	
Challenging	
Within Your Control	
Dynamic	
Performance	

What did I like? What do I want to keep for next time?

What do I want to find a solution for? Areas to change or improve?

New or Modified Performance Goal

Performance   Dynamic   Within Your Control   Challenging   Specific   Positive

Positive   Specific   Challenging   Within Your Control   Dynamic   Performance

Within Your Control   Challenging   Specific   Positive

Positive

Performance

Dynamic

Within Your Control

Challenging

Specific

Positive

Event	Date
Location	Time
Weather	Surface
Judge/Instructor	Dog

Performance Goal

Extent Achieved: 0 1 2 3 4 5 6 7 8 9 10

Challenge

Performance Strategy

Effectiveness: 0 1 2 3 4 5 6 7 8 9 10

SCT	YDS	Q/NQ	Place
Time	YPS	Points	Title

Notes			

Positive   Specific   Challenging   Within Your Control   Dynamic   Performance

Positive   Within Your Control   Challenging   Specific   Positive

 Clear Mind

Positive   Specific   Challenging   Within Your Control

What did I like? What do I want to keep for next time?

What do I want to find a solution for? Areas to change or improve?

New or Modified Performance Goal

Performance

Dynamic

Within Your Control

Challenging

Specific

Positive

Event	Date
Location	Time
Weather	Surface
Judge/Instructor	Dog

Performance Goal

Extent Achieved: 0 1 2 3 4 5 6 7 8 9 10

Challenge

Performance Strategy

Effectiveness: 0 1 2 3 4 5 6 7 8 9 10

SCT	YDS	Q/NQ	Place
Time	YPS	Points	Title
Notes			

Positive

Specific

Challenging

Within Your Control

Dynamic

Performance

Clear Mind

Positive   Specific   Challenging   Within Your Control

What did I like? What do I want to keep for next time?

What do I want to find a solution for? Areas to change or improve?

New or Modified Performance Goal

Event		Date	
Location		Time	
Weather		Surface	
Judge/Instructor		Dog	

Performance Goal

Extent Achieved: 0 1 2 3 4 5 6 7 8 9 10

Challenge

Performance Strategy

Effectiveness: 0 1 2 3 4 5 6 7 8 9 10

SCT	YDS	Q/NQ	Place
Time	YPS	Points	Title
Notes			

Positive   Specific   Challenging   Within Your Control

Positive	Performance	Dynamic	What did I like? What do I want to keep for next time?	Positive
Specific				Specific
Challenging	Within Your Control		What do I want to find a solution for? Areas to change or improve?	Challenging
Positive	Specific	Challenging	New or Modified Performance Goal	Within Your Control

What did I like? What do I want to keep for next time?

What do I want to find a solution for? Areas to change or improve?

New or Modified Performance Goal

Event	Date
Location	Time
Weather	Surface
Judge/Instructor	Dog

Performance Goal

Extent Achieved: 0 1 2 3 4 5 6 7 8 9 10

Challenge

Performance Strategy

Effectiveness: 0 1 2 3 4 5 6 7 8 9 10

SCT	YDS	Q/NQ	Place
Time	YPS	Points	Title

Notes			

Positive   Specific   Challenging   Within Your Control

What did I like? What do I want to keep for next time?

What do I want to find a solution for? Areas to change or improve?

New or Modified Performance Goal

Performance | Dynamic | Within Your Control | Challenging | Specific | Positive

Positive | Specific | Challenging | Within Your Control | Dynamic | Performance

Event	Date
Location	Time
Weather	Surface
Judge/Instructor	Dog

Performance Goal

Extent Achieved:　0　1　2　3　4　5　6　7　8　9　10

Challenge

Performance Strategy

Effectiveness:　0　1　2　3　4　5　6　7　8　9　10

SCT	YDS	Q/NQ	Place
Time	YPS	Points	Title

Notes			

Positive   Specific   Challenging   Within Your Control

What did I like? What do I want to keep for next time?
What do I want to find a solution for? Areas to change or improve?
New or Modified Performance Goal

Left margin (top to bottom): Performance   Dynamic   Within Your Control   Challenging   Specific   Positive

Right margin (top to bottom): Positive   Specific   Challenging   Within Your Control   Dynamic   Performance

Bottom margin: Within Your Control   Challenging   Specific   Positive

Event	Date
Location	Time
Weather	Surface
Judge/Instructor	Dog

Performance Goal

Extent Achieved: 0 1 2 3 4 5 6 7 8 9 10

Challenge

Performance Strategy

Effectiveness: 0 1 2 3 4 5 6 7 8 9 10

SCT	YDS	Q/NQ	Place
Time	YPS	Points	Title

Notes

Positive   Specific   Challenging   Within Your Control

What did I like? What do I want to keep for next time?

What do I want to find a solution for? Areas to change or improve?

New or Modified Performance Goal

Positive

Specific

Challenging

Within Your Control

Dynamic

Performance

Performance

Dynamic

Within Your Control

Challenging

Specific

Positive

Event		Date	
Location		Time	
Weather		Surface	
Judge/Instructor		Dog	

Performance Goal

Extent Achieved: 0 1 2 3 4 5 6 7 8 9 10

Challenge

Performance Strategy

Effectiveness: 0 1 2 3 4 5 6 7 8 9 10

SCT	YDS	Q/NQ	Place
Time	YPS	Points	Title

Notes

Positive   Specific   Challenging   Within Your Control

What did I like? What do I want to keep for next time?

What do I want to find a solution for? Areas to change or improve?

New or Modified Performance Goal

Positive
Performance

Dynamic

Within Your Control

Challenging

Specific

Positive

Event	Date
Location	Time
Weather	Surface
Judge/Instructor	Dog

Performance Goal

Extent Achieved: 0 1 2 3 4 5 6 7 8 9 10

Challenge

Performance Strategy

Effectiveness: 0 1 2 3 4 5 6 7 8 9 10

SCT	YDS	Q/NQ	Place
Time	YPS	Points	Title

Notes

Positive
Specific
Challenging
Within Your Control
Dynamic
Performance

  Clear Mind

Positive   Specific   Challenging   Within Your Control

What did I like? What do I want to keep for next time?

What do I want to find a solution for? Areas to change or improve?

New or Modified Performance Goal

Positive · Specific · Challenging · Within Your Control · Dynamic · Performance

Performance · Dynamic · Within Your Control · Challenging · Specific · Positive

Event	Date
Location	Time
Weather	Surface
Judge/Instructor	Dog

Performance Goal

Extent Achieved: 0   1   2   3   4   5   6   7   8   9   10

Challenge

Performance Strategy

Effectiveness: 0   1   2   3   4   5   6   7   8   9   10

SCT	YDS	Q/NQ	Place
Time	YPS	Points	Title

Notes

Positive   Specific   Challenging   Within Your Control

What did I like? What do I want to keep for next time?

What do I want to find a solution for? Areas to change or improve?

New or Modified Performance Goal

Positive

Performance

Specific

Dynamic

Challenging

Within Your Control

Within Your Control

Challenging

Dynamic

Specific

Performance

Positive

Event	Date
Location	Time
Weather	Surface
Judge/Instructor	Dog

Performance Goal

Extent Achieved: 0 1 2 3 4 5 6 7 8 9 10

Challenge

Performance Strategy

Effectiveness: 0 1 2 3 4 5 6 7 8 9 10

SCT	YDS	Q/NQ	Place
Time	YPS	Points	Title

Notes

Positive   Specific   Challenging   Within Your Control

What did I like? What do I want to keep for next time?

What do I want to find a solution for? Areas to change or improve?

New or Modified Performance Goal

Event	Date
Location	Time
Weather	Surface
Judge/Instructor	Dog

Performance Goal

Extent Achieved: 0 1 2 3 4 5 6 7 8 9 10

Challenge

Performance Strategy

Effectiveness: 0 1 2 3 4 5 6 7 8 9 10

SCT	YDS	Q/NQ	Place
Time	YPS	Points	Title

Notes

  Clear Mind

Positive   Specific   Challenging   Within Your Control

What did I like? What do I want to keep for next time?
What do I want to find a solution for? Areas to change or improve?
New or Modified Performance Goal

Positive   Specific   Challenging   Within Your Control

Event	Date
Location	Time
Weather	Surface
Judge/Instructor	Dog

Performance Goal

Extent Achieved: 0 1 2 3 4 5 6 7 8 9 10

Challenge

Performance Strategy

Effectiveness: 0 1 2 3 4 5 6 7 8 9 10

SCT	YDS	Q/NQ	Place
Time	YPS	Points	Title

Notes

Positive   Specific   Challenging   Within Your Control   Dynamic   Performance

Performance   Dynamic   Within Your Control   Challenging   Specific   Positive

Positive   Specific   Challenging   Within Your Control

What did I like? What do I want to keep for next time?

What do I want to find a solution for? Areas to change or improve?

New or Modified Performance Goal

Positive

Specific

Performance

Challenging

Dynamic

Within Your Control

Within Your Control

Dynamic

Challenging

Performance

Specific

Positive

Event		Date	
Location		Time	
Weather		Surface	
Judge/Instructor		Dog	

Performance Goal

Extent Achieved: 0 1 2 3 4 5 6 7 8 9 10

Challenge

Performance Strategy

Effectiveness: 0 1 2 3 4 5 6 7 8 9 10

SCT	YDS	Q/NQ	Place
Time	YPS	Points	Title

Notes			

Positive   Specific   Challenging   Within Your Control

What did I like? What do I want to keep for next time?

What do I want to find a solution for? Areas to change or improve?

New or Modified Performance Goal

Performance   Dynamic   Within Your Control   Challenging   Specific   Positive

Event	Date
Location	Time
Weather	Surface
Judge/Instructor	Dog

Performance Goal

Extent Achieved: 0 1 2 3 4 5 6 7 8 9 10

Challenge

Performance Strategy

Effectiveness: 0 1 2 3 4 5 6 7 8 9 10

SCT	YDS	Q/NQ	Place
Time	YPS	Points	Title

Notes

Positive   Specific   Challenging   Within Your Control   Dynamic   Performance

Clear Mind

Positive   Specific   Challenging   Within Your Control

What did I like? What do I want to keep for next time?

What do I want to find a solution for? Areas to change or improve?

New or Modified Performance Goal

Event	Date
Location	Time
Weather	Surface
Judge/Instructor	Dog

Performance Goal

Extent Achieved: 0 1 2 3 4 5 6 7 8 9 10

Challenge

Performance Strategy

Effectiveness: 0 1 2 3 4 5 6 7 8 9 10

SCT	YDS	Q/NQ	Place
Time	YPS	Points	Title

Notes

 Clear Mind

Positive   Specific   Challenging   Within Your Control

What did I like? What do I want to keep for next time?

What do I want to find a solution for? Areas to change or improve?

New or Modified Performance Goal

Positive   Specific   Challenging   Within Your Control   Dynamic   Performance

Performance   Dynamic   Within Your Control   Challenging   Specific   Positive

Event	Date
Location	Time
Weather	Surface
Judge/Instructor	Dog

Performance Goal

Extent Achieved: 0   1   2   3   4   5   6   7   8   9   10

Challenge

Performance Strategy

Effectiveness: 0   1   2   3   4   5   6   7   8   9   10

SCT	YDS	Q/NQ	Place
Time	YPS	Points	Title

Notes

Positive   Specific   Challenging   Within Your Control

What did I like? What do I want to keep for next time?	
What do I want to find a solution for? Areas to change or improve?	
New or Modified Performance Goal	

Performance   Dynamic   Within Your Control   Challenging   Specific   Positive

Positive   Specific   Challenging   Within Your Control   Dynamic   Performance

Positive   Specific   Challenging   Within Your Control

Event	Date
Location	Time
Weather	Surface
Judge/Instructor	Dog

Performance Goal

Extent Achieved: 0 1 2 3 4 5 6 7 8 9 10

Challenge

Performance Strategy

Effectiveness: 0 1 2 3 4 5 6 7 8 9 10

SCT	YDS	Q/NQ	Place
Time	YPS	Points	Title

Notes

Clear Mind

Positive   Specific   Challenging   Within Your Control

What did I like? What do I want to keep for next time?	
What do I want to find a solution for? Areas to change or improve?	
New or Modified Performance Goal	

(Left margin, top to bottom: Performance, Dynamic, Within Your Control, Challenging, Specific, Positive)

(Right margin, top to bottom: Positive, Specific, Challenging, Within Your Control, Dynamic, Performance)

(Bottom margin, inverted: Within Your Control, Challenging, Specific, Positive)

MORE RESOURCES AVAILABLE AT
www.daisypeel.com

- *Blog*
- *eBooks*
- *Online Learning*
- *Seminars*
- *Instructional Videos*
- *Helpful Links*
- *Other Websites By Daisy Creative*

Follow Daisy on FACEBOOK

—

Made in the USA
Lexington, KY
06 May 2015